Lynn's Itchy Skin:

Beautiful with Eczema

Outside and In

Published by
Queen V Publishing
Englewood, OH
QueenVPublishing.com

Queen V Publishing
Englewood, OH
QueenVPublishing.com

Copyright ©2021 by April Lynn Foster

Library of Congress Control Number: 2021902491

ISBN-13: 978-0-9962991-4-5

Illustrations by Sashai Dean

Edited by Valerie J. Lewis Coleman

Printed in the U.S.

This book belongs to

_____

Lynn has eczema, which makes her skin very itchy. To help her feel better, her mother gives her oatmeal baths and uses aloe Vera cooling lotion. Her mother keeps her in cool places and rubs bananas on her skin when it's red and puffy.

When the itching is really bad, Lynn's mother mixes a little honey with aloe Vera so it's not sticky. She rubs the gel on Lynn's eczema spots. Oatmeal, aloe Vera, bananas and honey are natural healers that reduce pain, cool the skin and stop itching.

Her mother said, "Lynn, you are beautiful. Stay hopeful that your skin will feel better."

Lynn and her best friend, Loren, find indoor activities when Lynn's eczema bothers her. Loren sticks by her best friend whenever she is not feeling well. They love to laugh and watch movies like *The Best Friends Vacation* series. Lynn keeps her special lotion nearby in case her skin starts to itch.

Many foods cause Lynn's skin to itch, burn, swell and sometimes bleed. Oranges, dairy milk, eggs and tomatoes are the worse. If she uses hot water, her skin gets red and puffy because she scratches so much. Sometimes, Lynn has to visit the dermatologist or skin doctor.

Lynn said, "My skin still turns red and burns. I scratch so much that my skin tears and bleeds."

The doctor said, "Stay away from scented things. They smell nice, but hurt your skin. Keep using cooling lotions and avoid the bad foods we talked about." He gave her mother a prescription. "This cortisone cream should help stop her open sores and scabs from itching. If this cream doesn't work, we have other treatments including ultraviolet phototherapy."

Lynn's mother said, "Ultraviolet phototherapy?"

"It's a light treatment that helps stop the itching. It looks like a stand-up tanning bed." He looked at Lynn. "I'll do my best to help the itching and irritation go away. I want you to try your best not to scratch because it causes scarring and marks. Okay?"

Lynn nodded.

Over summer break, Lynn and Loren spend lots of time together. To avoid breakouts, Lynn plans her meals, activities and outfits when she visits. She packs her lunch and long-sleeve shirts in case her skin itches. The shirts help her feel more comfortable because people cannot stare at her skin.

One day, Loren had spaghetti for lunch. Lynn ate vegetable soup and a sandwich because spaghetti sauce flares up the eczema around her mouth. The girls talked about all the fun things they were going to do while they enjoyed different lunches.

Lynn and her parents discovered that when she ate plant-based meals, her skin felt better. She ate very little meat and junk food. Natural products and fresh, organic veggies reduced her eczema flare-ups. Instead of dairy products like cow milk, Lynn switched to oat and rice milks. Plant milk is another option and if you do not have nut allergies, almond or cashew milk are pretty good.

Loren enjoys helping her mother plant flowers and maintain her garden.

Loren said, "Mommy, Lynn has itchy skin and it hurts her sometimes. I don't like her skin to hurt. She gets sad sometimes because her skin is different. Her mother said that aloe Vera helps her itching. Can we give her one of the aloe Vera plants from your garden?"

"Sure, Loren. That is so nice of you to want to make your best friend feel better."

Loren and her mother visited Lynn's family. They gave them an aloe Vera plant to help Lynn's eczema.

Lynn's mother said, "Thank you. I will scoop out the aloe Vera gel from a leaf and put it in a blender to make a lotion for her itchy spots."

Loren smiled.

Lynn said, "When I rub my special lotion on the eczema, it cools my skin, stops the pain and makes me feel better."

Lynn wanted to play outside with the other kids, but the sun bothered her skin.

When it's hot outside, Lynn and Loren find fun things to do inside the house. They enjoy many indoor activities including dancing, playing Twister and listening to music.

For more indoor fun, Lynn and Loren make a tent in her bedroom. They pretend to be princesses in a castle. They eat popsicles Lynn's mother made from fresh fruit, drink mango juice with ice to keep Lynn's skin cool and read books.

Lynn's Dos and Don'ts

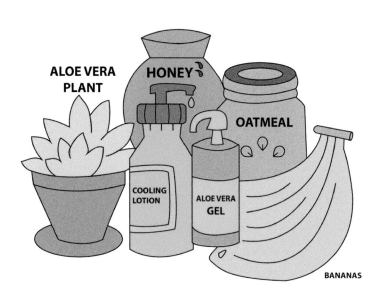

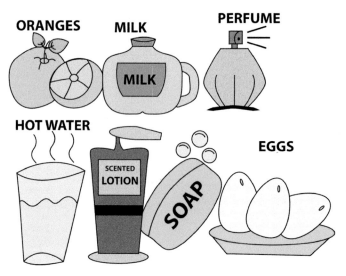

Lynn's Dos and Don'ts

Dos

- Eat a plant-based diet
- Keep your skin hydrated with natural creams and lotions
- Ask your dermatologist which treatment is best for you from hundreds of topical creams, ointments, injections and even ultraviolent light.

Don'ts

- Eat or drink dairy products including milk chocolate
- Eat too much meat or tomato sauce
- Sit in the sun too long
- Use scented products
- Use hot water

As an adult, Lynn still eats a plant-based diet and uses her homemade Lynn's Creations Cream daily. Plant-based soaps, laundry detergents and deodorants help her avoid flare-ups.

Do you have eczema or know someone who does?

What happens when the skin itches?

What can you do to help?

What foods help eczema?

What foods hurt eczema?

Lynn's Itchy Skin Seek-n-Find

For added fun, try *Lynn's Itchy Skin Seek-n-Find*.
Use a red crayon or marker for Lynn's eczema triggers.
Use blue for eczema remedies Lynn used.

Triggers

Dairy
Hot Water
Oranges
Perfumes
Sun
Tomato

Remedies

Aloe Vera
Bananas
Honey
Oatmeal
Rice Milk
Veggies

O	I	H	V	E	G	G	I	E	S	S
R	N	O	O	T	E	L	C	S	Y	O
A	B	T	E	T	C	R	U	B	L	A
N	E	W	R	O	E	I	R	A	B	T
G	G	A	S	M	E	C	C	N	F	M
E	H	T	L	A	U	E	E	A	A	E
S	Y	E	T	T	P	M	O	N	Q	A
K	N	R	Z	O	H	I	O	A	E	L
D	F	N	B	U	N	L	A	S	Y	L
A	L	S	U	N	E	K	A	K	N	H
I	L	P	E	V	E	Q	W	U	O	O
R	C	P	E	R	F	U	M	E	S	N
Y	N	V	I	Q	S	E	A	O	A	E
A	A	L	O	E	V	E	R	A	C	Y

No Itch Zone

Lynn's Recommended Resources

To soothe and hydrate your eczema skin, visit LynnsItchySkin.com for her special creams, lotions and scrubs.

Visit these sites for more information about eczema:

Eczema.com

NationalEczema.org

AAD.org/public/diseases/eczema